MAGNIFICENT DESOLATION

poems by

Heather Cox

Finishing Line Press
Georgetown, Kentucky

MAGNIFICENT DESOLATION

ACKNOWLEDGMENTS

Thank you to the editors of the following publications where some of these
poems first appeared: *Columbia Poetry Review, Midwestern Gothic, Moon City
Review, Pear Noir!,* and *Used Furniture Review.*

Thank you to Joshua Poteat for the line "we did / what we could to keep the
world ours" from which I borrow in "Letter Left of the Cusp of our Favorite
Crater."

Thank you to Frank Rogaczewski, Kathleen Rooney, and Kyle Beachy, whose
guidance was crucial to the shaping of this chapbook.

And to Rachel, whose enduring support is crucial to everything.

Publisher: Leah Maines

Editor: Christen Kincaid

Cover Art and Design: Heather Cox

Author Photo: Heather Cox

Printed in the USA on acid-free paper.
Order online: www.finishinglinepress.com
            also available on amazon.com

Author inquiries and mail orders:
Finishing Line Press
P. O. Box 1626
Georgetown, Kentucky 40324
U. S. A.

Table of Contents

"It suddenly struck me that that tiny pea, pretty and blue,
was the Earth. I put up my thumb and shut one eye,
and my thumb blotted out the planet Earth.
I didn't feel like a giant.
I felt very, very small."
—Neil Armstrong

"Beautiful, beautiful. Magnificent Desolation."
—Buzz Aldrin

We Were Tired of Living on Earth

I.

The wood panels on the wall began to flake and splinter.
We saw, more than once, the face of Jesus Christ
in carpet stains. The ceiling dripped syrup; the vents
coughed black ash.

Our neighbors never smiled—in face, I can't remember
their full faces, only frowns.

Our yard, a patch of crippled grass, lasted only
a single spring rain before remaining a mudpuddle.

We heard the moon was made of cheese and the cost
of living, cheap.

II.

We started sleeping in tents, poking strings of lights
through our tarp roof to build our own constellations.

The moon shone through
when the fuses blew.

Our stomachs taut as tightrope,
we planned our exodus. Our knuckles
cracked, our fingernails chipped, our exhausted arms
drooped as we built a small rocketship
from fragments of our life on earth: engines, tires,
copper springs, gold coils, aluminum foil
and siding, garden hoses, telescopes.

We sparked through the night unnoticed,
save a few neighbors we never knew anyway.

Into the Magnificent Desolation

I.

We don't know much about gravity
but we sense a dark energy
nuzzle the nape of our necks

stretching our shadows
that sprout from the light
of a single swinging bulb

and against its will
we float closer together.

Out the one window, streaks of street lights
dim and we drift out of atmosphere.

Scrambled broadcasts might spring
from satellites obeying orbits,
but silence is all we hear from here.

II.

The moon occupies our wider horizon,
flashlight under our blanket of sky.

Its scorched skin startles us, but
its myriad dimples delight;

we imagine tickling them with our toes
as we stare back at that former planet.

Our new vantage gives us perspective:
we were so small before, a fraction

of a fraction, the piece of the pie so insignificant
it's left untouched after dinner. Soon,

we will be alpha and omega, an entire population
microscopic, eager to occupy

this most miraculous acreage alone.

III.

We wonder what our presence
on the moon will disturb.

Will earth's oceans' tides
flatline, unrevived?

Will we accelerate global warming?
Bring forth a new freeze?

Will the night be a smidgen darker
due to the stain of our silhouettes?

Would such a dimming
stifle dreaming? Stifle wonderment?

Will all our own questions
be answered? Or multiplied?

First Night on the Moon

We could have chattered
about how the cosmos

is more than caramel-centered
candy bars, how much

I'd like you to slip
one of Saturn's rings

around my finger, how
we reach for revolution,

but spin in the exact
orbit always. We could have

talked about the universe,
but we just stared at stars

streaking and blew smoke
rings in our mind because

we forgot to bring the pot.

Second Night on the Moon

We spoon in our rocketship,
and the buttons of my flannel

temporarily tattoo your skin paler
than the moon. I dream you ask:

How can these planets exist
without exploding?

How do we spin around the sun
without a visible tether?

Where in this emptiness
exists dark forces we can't see?

When I wake I remember
ancient gods from our old world

and I wonder if from here,
without atmospheric

interference, *I* could keep
all existence in balance.

Master of the Universe

I slouch in the comfiest
of craters, crack my knuckles back,

preparing to work my magic. I
inhale, stealing the smell

of night from the flat air.
I touch my lips to the ether,

mouthing words to rouse the earth—
light, worship, dominion—

I use my mute tongue
as a rope to tug the planets

along their invisible
heliocentric orbit.

It looks like it's working.

Earth, Pshh.

I close my eyes and imagine sunset,
painted tangerine and plum
rotting into night.

The sky nothing
but miles of asphalt; we don't need
pedestrian things

like dusk or dawn.
Here, we are earth's
beacon, we rise

the tides, we are mother
nature, gravity
locked-in. Here,

great lakes are filled
with basalts, lava leftovers,
fancier than freshwater

and fish. We can swim
in space if we
really want to.

We are closer
to the sun
sometimes.

Third Night on the Moon

We have been trying to exist
better than we did before,

but there's no way to tell
if the grass is greener

on this chalk rock, and all
we do is doodle in the dust:

trinkets we used to tinker
with, records we used to spin,

clothes we'd worn 'til the fabric
unfurled in a nest of fray.

You had asked before

*What will we do when we run
out of things to say?*

We sit without speaking,

because by now we know this cold
rock snuffs out every sound.

Fever Dreams

We're in a field of flames that keep sprouting like corn. They spread like melting butter, bubbling then popping. Your toes turn black and toast into ash. The wind coughs charred dust and it fades into the pale white of stars.

We're in a field of flames that won't stop crackling. You're spreading ash onto your toast. The wind blends the black of night and the white of stars.

A field of flames. You're burning stars.

Remember

those nights sticking to my tongue the sour of whiskey—
I am trying to remember—

these husks shucking clothing we were hiding—
I am trying—

swallowing starry nights chasing with wine our instincts—
to remember—

tongues approaching midnight swirling one constellation—
come closer—

nova kiss pillow pressed sheet sweat holding you—
I am trying—

Lunar Aubade

It's 5 a.m. somewhere,
but it's always midnight

here. A star winks slightly
some light years away

hoping we'll still be around
to see it in the future.

In this darkness you don't notice,
as I unravel myself from you,

tiny dust clouds accumulating
before I skip away. I'd leave a note

but I'll be in this same rock-
bed tomorrow

for the rest of my life.

On the Moon, Every Month is December

I.

The dust begins to settle at what would be dusk,
shrinking tighter like the tucking of a blanket.

When we were younger
we thought the man in moon

might roll us in his mouth
before chewing us like gum drops.
Now, we fog the scuffed glass
window with our breath,

looking out at powdered pinnacles
and darkened craters—the pocks

like lonely scars no one ever touches
to remember. We ask ourselves

*What memories should we keep? How
should we move on?*

until the answers scramble in our mind
so many times we ignore the questions.

II.

Beyond the absence of atmosphere
frail whispers rub brittle like bone,

words waiting to snap in half, waiting
to separate like when lightning
would crack the sky into pieces. I only
wish for fragments through the night,

for the tiniest ripple of waves
in a creek bed, on a radio,

but memory shuffles
each sentence before

it slinks in my ear. I think I hear
hollow shell

or *frozen hell,* maybe *empty arms*
or *lover's swarm* or *broken charm.* I think

I feel a sinking, a deepening
of night, a shrinking of distant light

before I'm shuttered back by
your rank breath.

Lines Composed in a Crater

I.

You cradle the meteorites
that fall beside your feet.

I wonder why the sky
would throw such things.

My bones rattle cold when
we count wrinkles in the moon.

II.

I am floating farther away
from your warmth.

When I orbit you, I no
longer scorch at the edges.

They will say of you:
She once contained life.

They will say of me:
data inconclusive.

New Kind of Letter

I try writing to you in blood, so you can better see the letters, but the blood begins to tell another story. When I write *love* the platelets part and their absence says *obligation*. I tell you that I'll never leave you, I write *forever*, but it reads *evaporate*, then *vanish*. I get tired of trying to tell you the truth and I sign my name anyway but the letters spell *no one*.

Lunacy

There would be something in the water
if this rock had springs or lakes—at least rain—
but it's so dry it's only dust
and that leaves us with what excuse?

If this place had lakes or rivers
would we swallow all the water and sink?
We wouldn't leave a note, an excuse.
We'd drift into silt in silence.

Some days I swallow my thoughts and sink
into darkness—it sparks a madness.
I drift into a silt of silence,
but my mind is buzzing like beehive.

Cosmonauts know this darkness is madness.
No blue skies, no rising sun,
no small sounds like buzzing from beehive,
nothing but the noise of your own thoughts.

No blue skies, no rising sun, no Starbucks—
all the things we knew are lost to us now.
Our only comfort is the sound of our own thoughts,
repeating endlessly like lines in a pantoum.

Everything we knew is lost.
It's so dry, we're full of dust.
Blank land repeats endlessly, a flatline.
There must be something in the water.

Myths about the Moon

The meteor showers
aren't that bad; the view
is worth it.

It's fun to bounce around
in a fraction of the Earth's gravity,
not at all nauseating.

The moon is a sleeping
satellite so distant
its influence on us
is irrelevant, if not
nonexistent.

There is no dark side
to the moon,
no sinister smile.

The moon is made of cheese.

Truths about the Moon

The view of Earth rising
is, of course, unparalleled.

The view of everything else
is pretty shitty.

You don't need a raincoat,
though an umbrella might help
with all the falling
fragments of space junk.

The moon is a spoon
that stirs the water of Earth
inside us;

some Tums
would come in handy.

There is no cheese here, nothing
to fill any appetite.

Letter Left on the Cusp of Our Favorite Crater

It's been weeks
of no talking, no texting, no music, no
television or internet.

I thought we would be
the center of the universe,
the mini-moon colony on a hill.

I thought the egg-crate
would have been more comfortable.

I thought the sex
would have been better.

It's been weeks
and we're still the only things
to look at.

I told you not to
forget your makeup.

We did what we could
to make this world ours,

but fingerdrawn notes in dust
are so hard to read with these
dried out contact lenses.

This is all to say
I'm taking the [rocketship] house,

but you can have the moon.
I think we both know

who's getting the better deal here.

PS:

Whenever you decide
to fall back into our atmosphere,

I hope you land close enough
for me to collect your ashes.

Heather Cox is the founding editor of *Ghost Ocean Magazine* and the handmade chapbook press Tree Light Books. Her poetry has been published in *Barrelhouse, Bodega, Indiana Review, The Pinch, Pinwheel, RHINO,* and elsewhere, while her interviews and reviews have been published in *Chicago Review of Books, Ghost Ocean, Mid-American Review,* and *Toad Suck Review.* She is the author of two other chapbooks, *Mole People* (BatCat Press) and *Echolocation* (dancing girl press). An Arkansas native, Heather spent the better half of the last decade living in Chicago, where she was awarded a Luminarts Cultural Foundation of Chicago fellowship. She now lives in northern Colorado with her wife and their two dogs and can be found online at looklookhere.tumblr.com.